ED EMBERLEY'S GREAT THUMBPRINT DRAWING BOOK

LITTLE, BROWN AND COMPANY · BOSTON · NEW YORK · LONDON

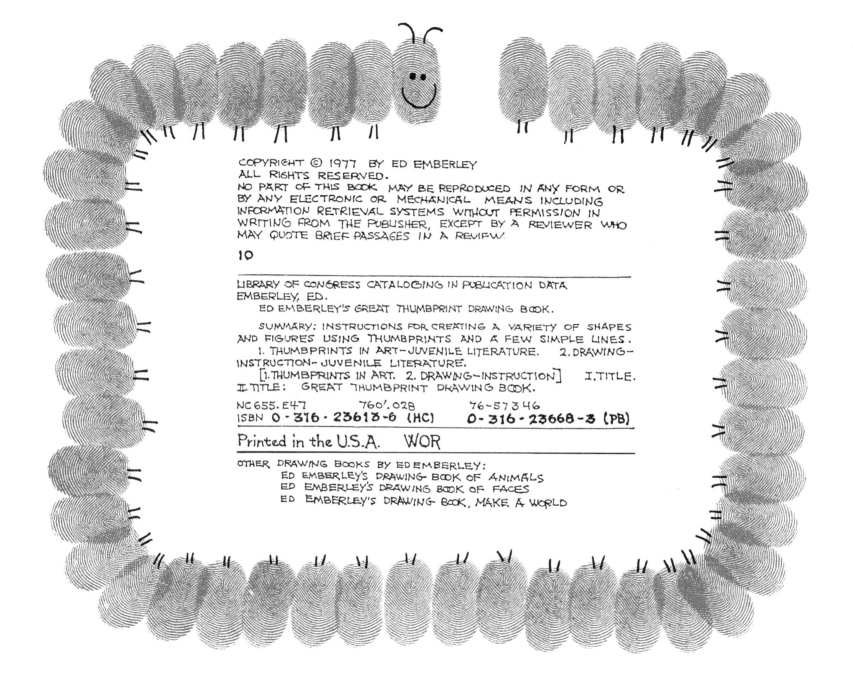

LIBRARY OF CONGRESS CATALOGING IN PUBLICATION DATA
EMBERLEY, ED.
    ED EMBERLEY'S GREAT THUMBPRINT DRAWING BOOK.

    SUMMARY: INSTRUCTIONS FOR CREATING A VARIETY OF SHAPES
AND FIGURES USING THUMBPRINTS AND A FEW SIMPLE LINES.
    1. THUMBPRINTS IN ART—JUVENILE LITERATURE.   2. DRAWING—
INSTRUCTION— JUVENILE LITERATURE.
    [1.THUMBPRINTS IN ART. 2. DRAWING—INSTRUCTION]   I.TITLE.
II.TITLE: GREAT THUMBPRINT DRAWING BOOK.

NC655.E47   760'.028   76-57346
ISBN 0·316·23613-6 (HC)   0·316·23668-3 (PB)

Printed in the U.S.A.   WOR

OTHER DRAWING BOOKS BY ED EMBERLEY:
        ED EMBERLEY'S DRAWING BOOK OF ANIMALS
        ED EMBERLEY'S DRAWING BOOK OF FACES
        ED EMBERLEY'S DRAWING BOOK, MAKE A WORLD

WHERE TO FIND IT PAGE

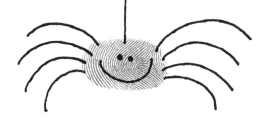

THIS BOOK SHOWS HOW TO DRAW PICTURES.
USING THIS NAME AND THUMBPRINTS.

iVY LOU

FOR INSTANCE,
THESE LETTERS PLUS THIS PRINT MAKE THIS BIRD!

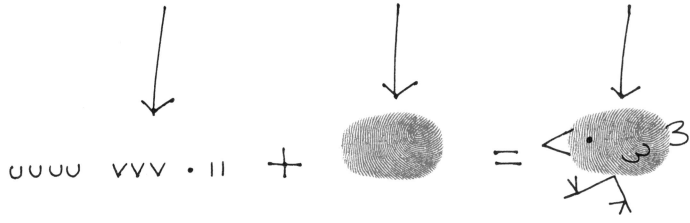

THIS ROW SHOWS
WHAT TO DRAW.

THIS ROW SHOWS
WHERE TO PUT IT.

3

THERE WILL BE:
LETTERS TURNED AROUND,
SCRIBBLES,
AND FILLING IN.

(THIS SIGN MEANS FILL IN → ﬡ)

4

FOR INSTANCE

PERSON (MORE FOLKS ON PAGE 9)

(JUST A LINE CAN MAKE A HAT.)

WALKING (MORE ACTION ON PAGE 15)

5

FISH (MORE CRITTERS ON PAGE 20)

BIRD (MORE BIRDS ON PAGE 24)

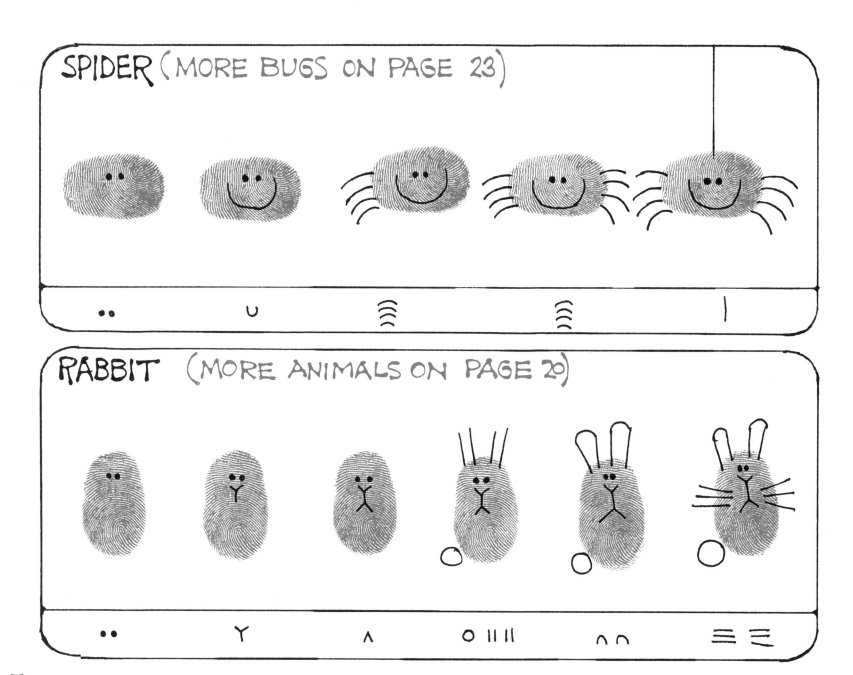

SPIDER (MORE BUGS ON PAGE 23)

RABBIT (MORE ANIMALS ON PAGE 20)

HALLOWEEN (MORE HOLIDAYS ON PAGE 26)

FROG (MORE THINGS WITH 2 THUMBPRINTS ON PAGE 31)

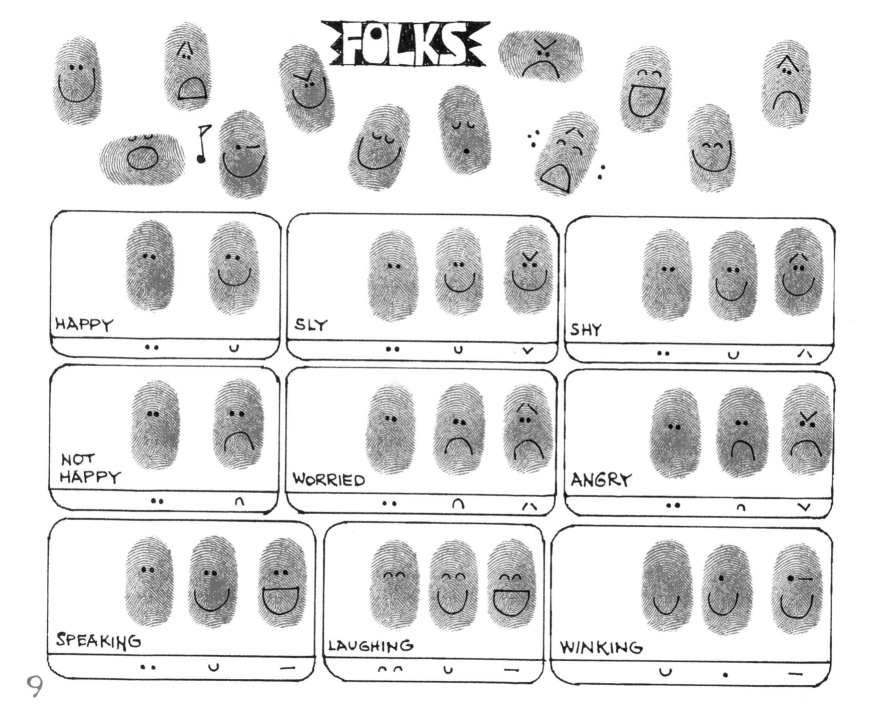

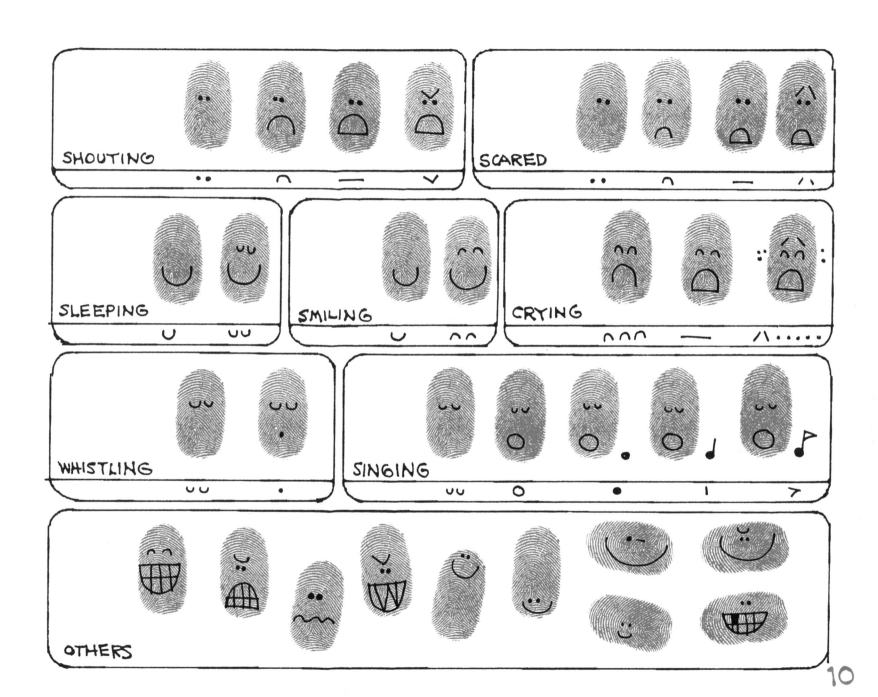

SHOUTING

SCARED

SLEEPING

SMILING

CRYING

WHISTLING

SINGING

OTHERS

10

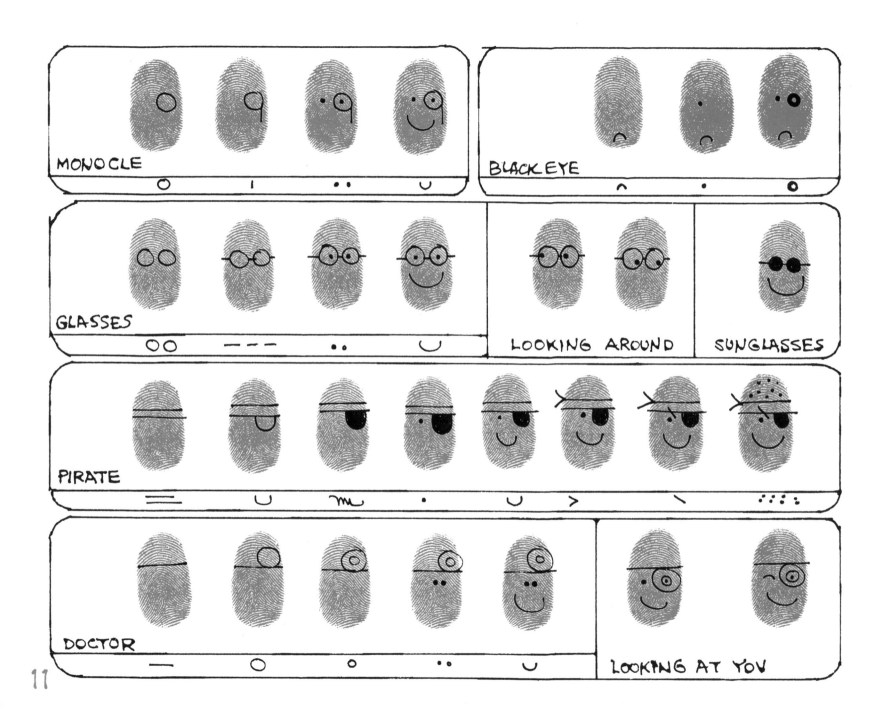

MONOCLE

BLACK EYE

GLASSES

LOOKING AROUND

SUNGLASSES

PIRATE

DOCTOR

LOOKING AT YOU

11

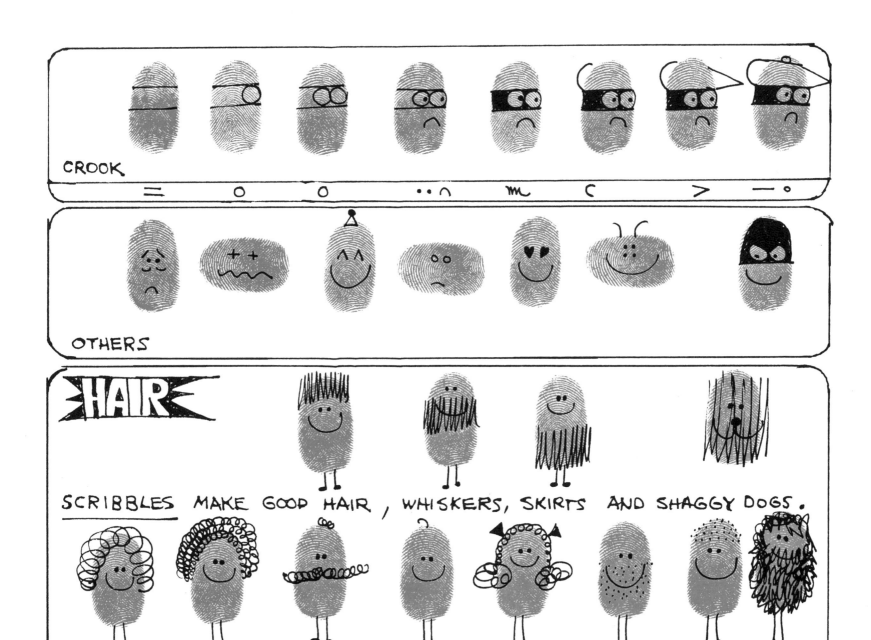

CROOK

OTHERS

HAIR

SCRIBBLES MAKE GOOD HAIR, WHISKERS, SKIRTS AND SHAGGY DOGS.

HERE ARE SOME MORE SCRIBBLES AND SOME SPECKS AND SCRATCHES.

12

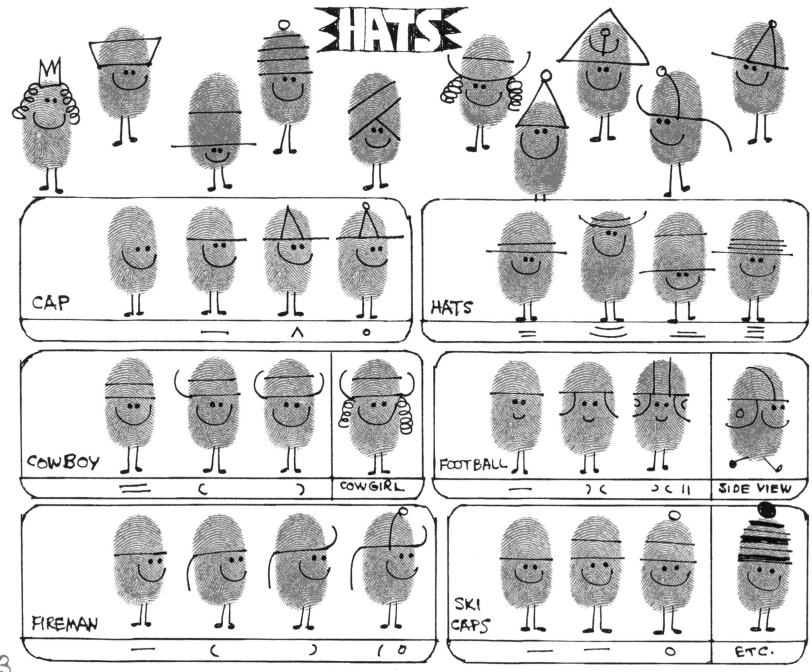

HATS

CAP

HATS

COWBOY — ( ) COWGIRL

FOOTBALL —)( )(|| SIDE VIEW

FIREMAN — ( ) (0

SKI CAPS — — 0 ETC.

13

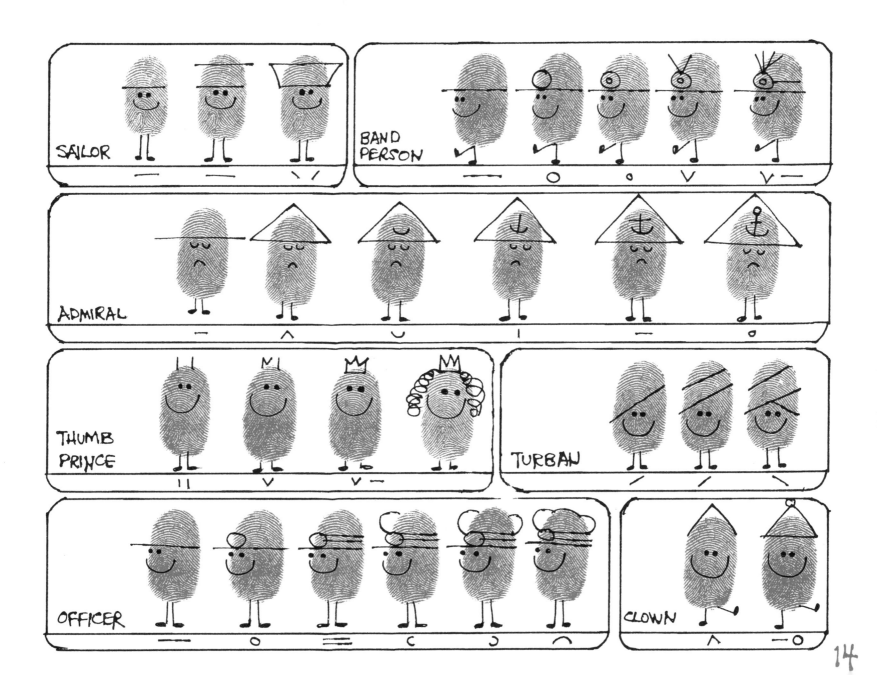

SAILOR

BAND PERSON

ADMIRAL

THUMB PRINCE

TURBAN

OFFICER

CLOWN

14

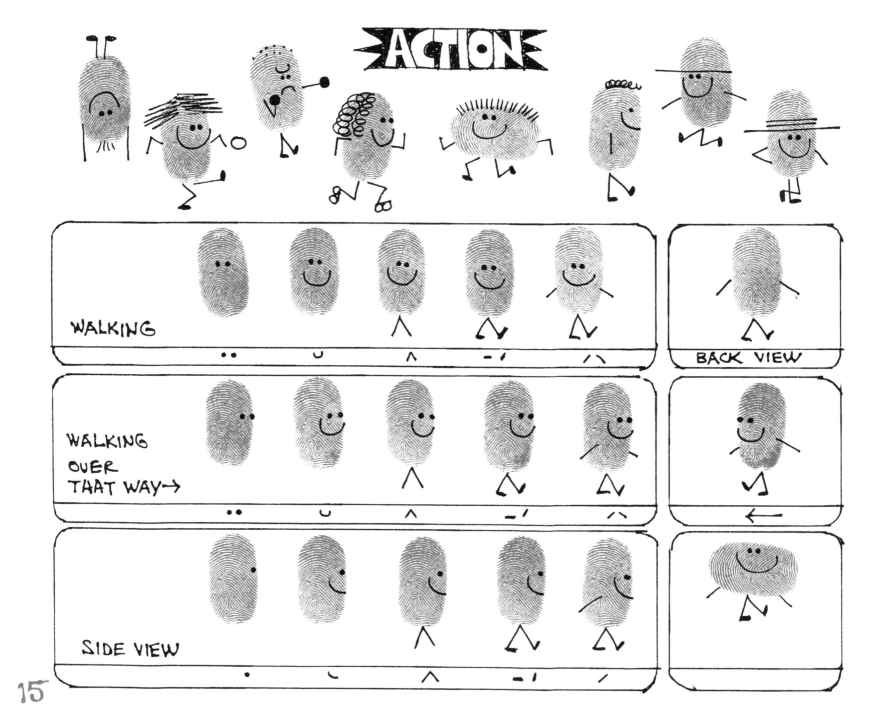

ACTION

WALKING

BACK VIEW

WALKING OVER THAT WAY →

SIDE VIEW

15

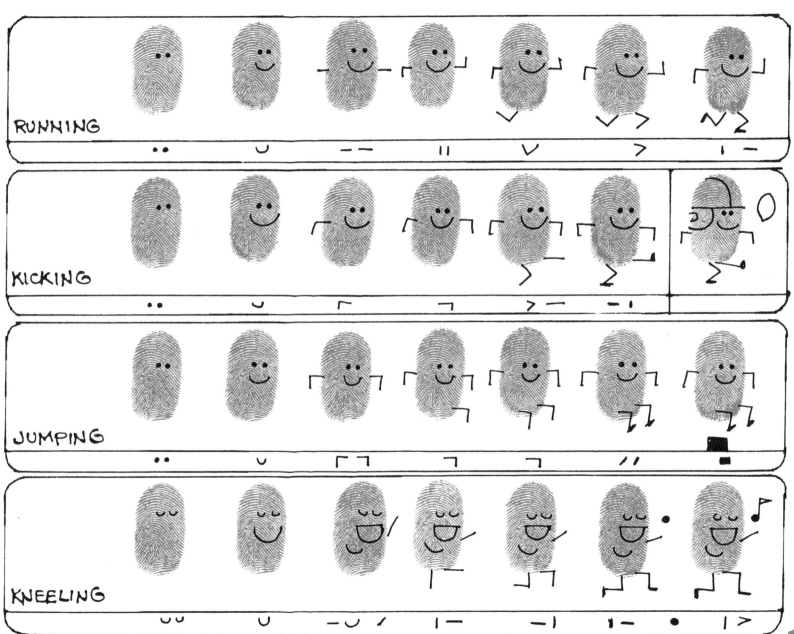

RUNNING

KICKING

JUMPING

KNEELING

16

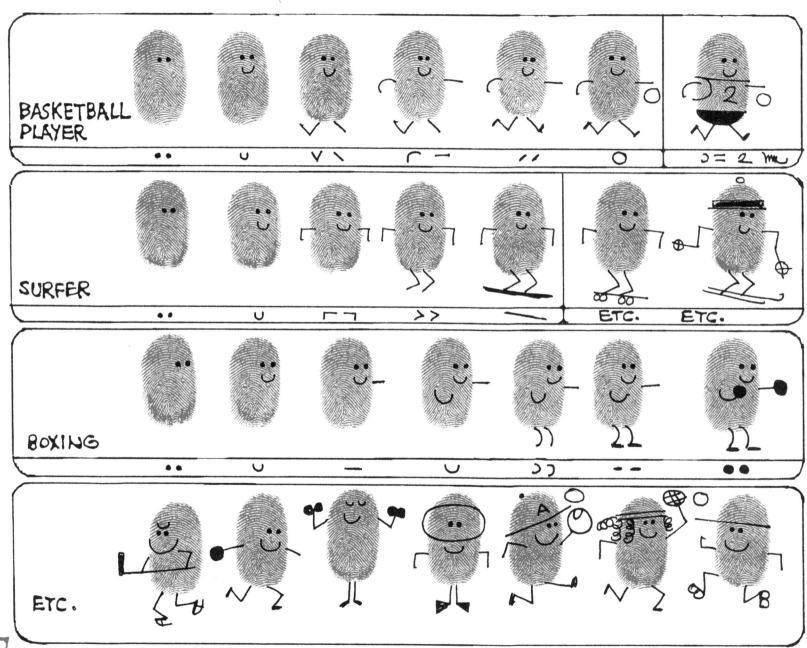

BASKETBALL
PLAYER

SURFER

BOXING

ETC.

17

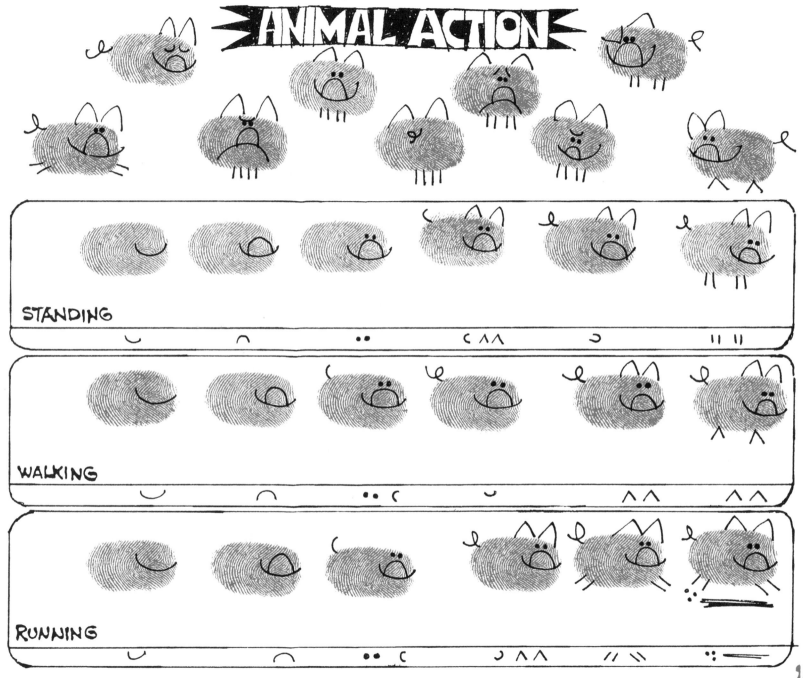

ANIMAL ACTION

STANDING

WALKING

RUNNING

18

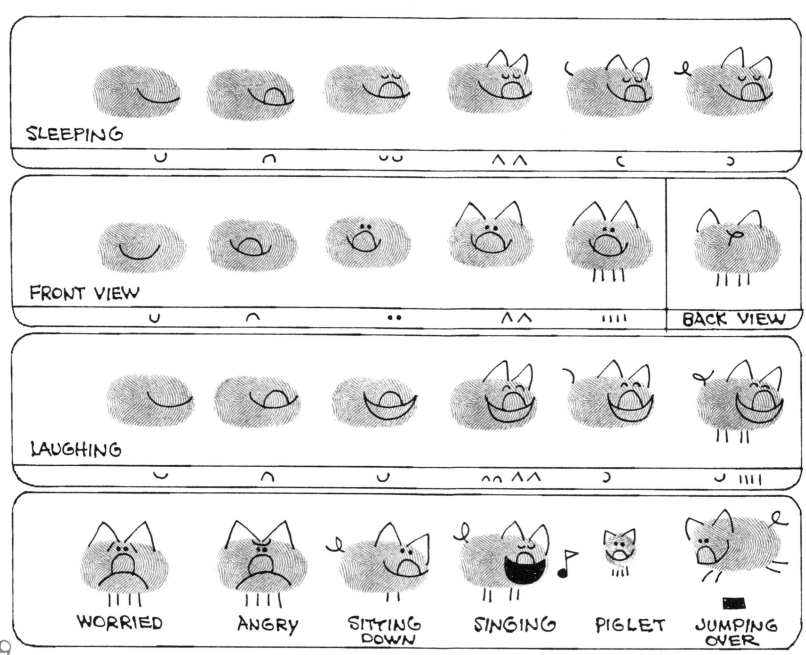

SLEEPING

⌣ ⌒ ⌣⌣ ʌʌ C ɔ

FRONT VIEW

⌣ ⌒ •• ʌʌ ||||

BACK VIEW

LAUGHING

⌣ ⌒ ⌣ ⌒⌒ ʌʌ ɔ ⌣ ||||

WORRIED   ANGRY   SITTING   SINGING   PIGLET   JUMPING
                     DOWN   OVER

19

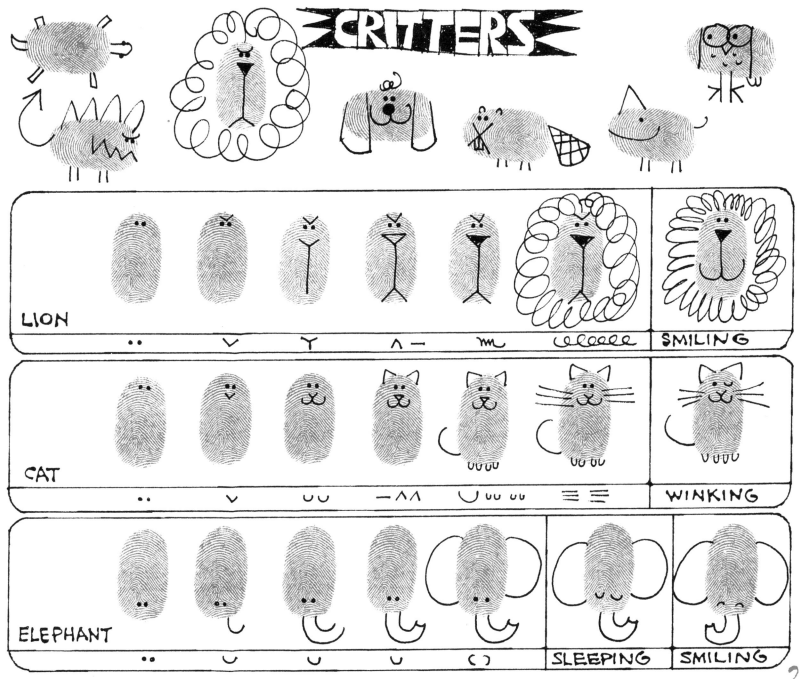

CRITTERS

LION

SMILING

CAT

WINKING

ELEPHANT

SLEEPING   SMILING

20

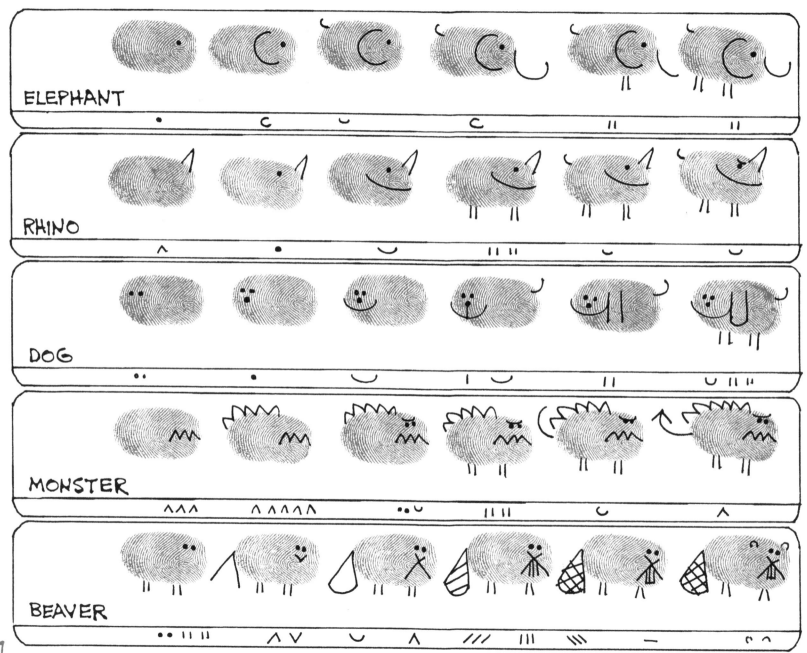

ELEPHANT

RHINO

DOG

MONSTER

BEAVER

21

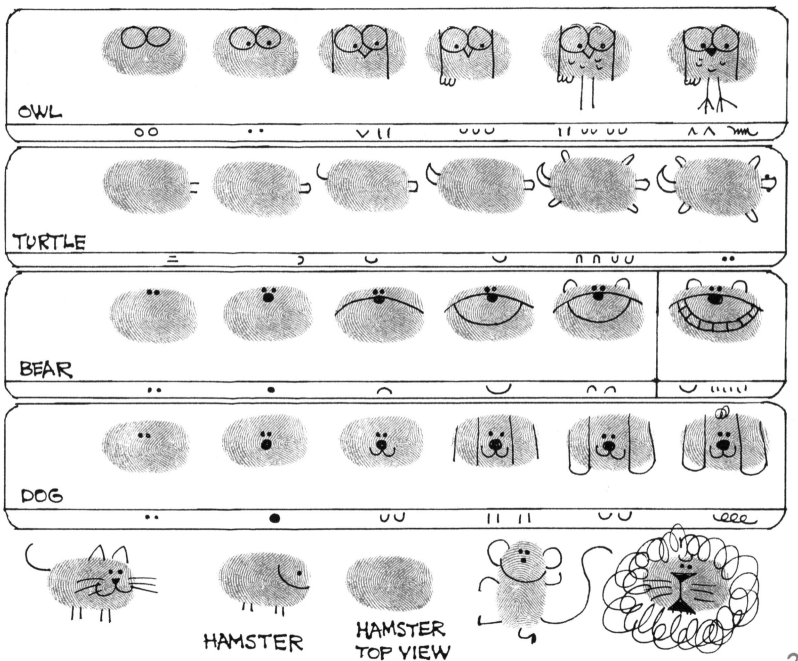

OWL

TURTLE

BEAR

DOG

HAMSTER

HAMSTER
TOP VIEW

22

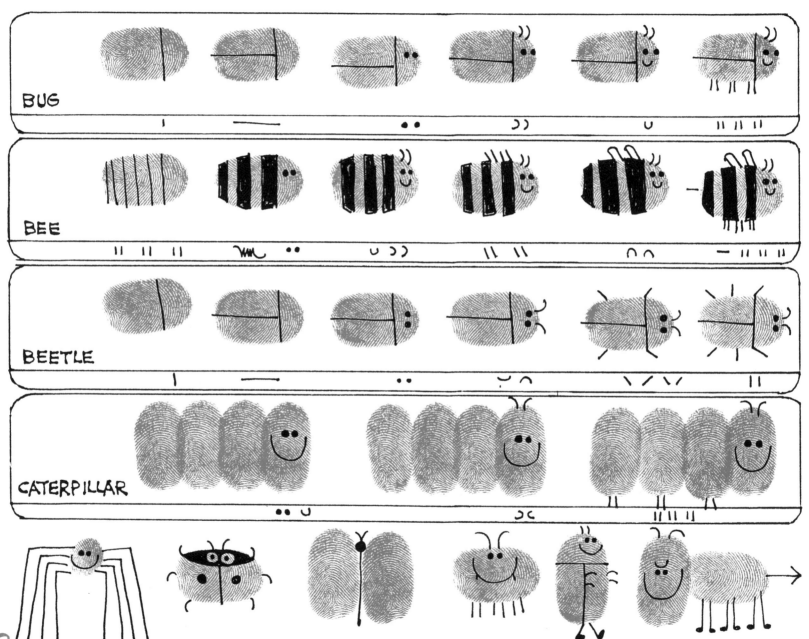

BUG

BEE

BEETLE

CATERPILLAR

23

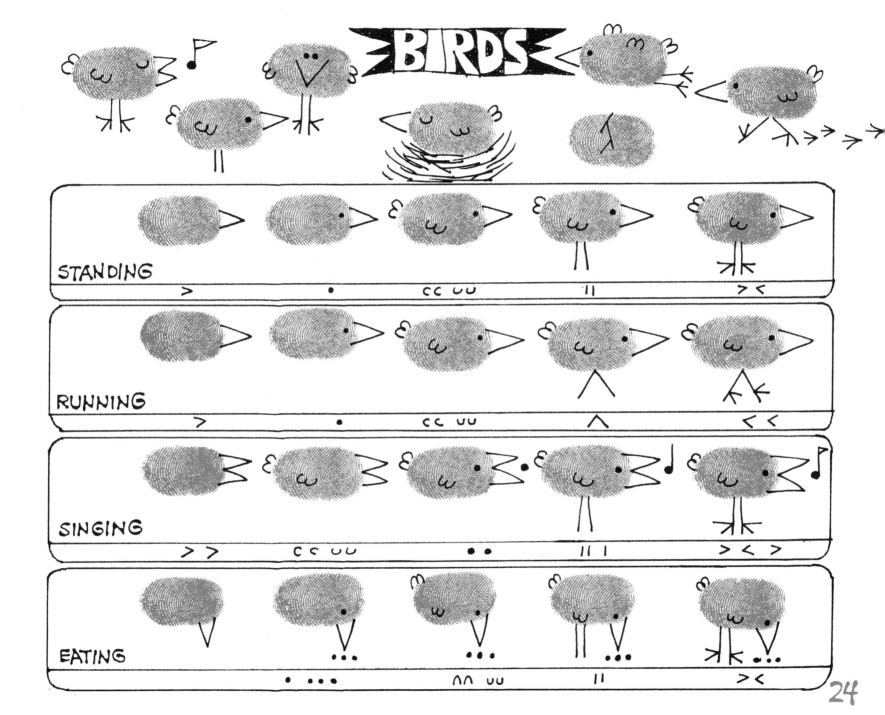

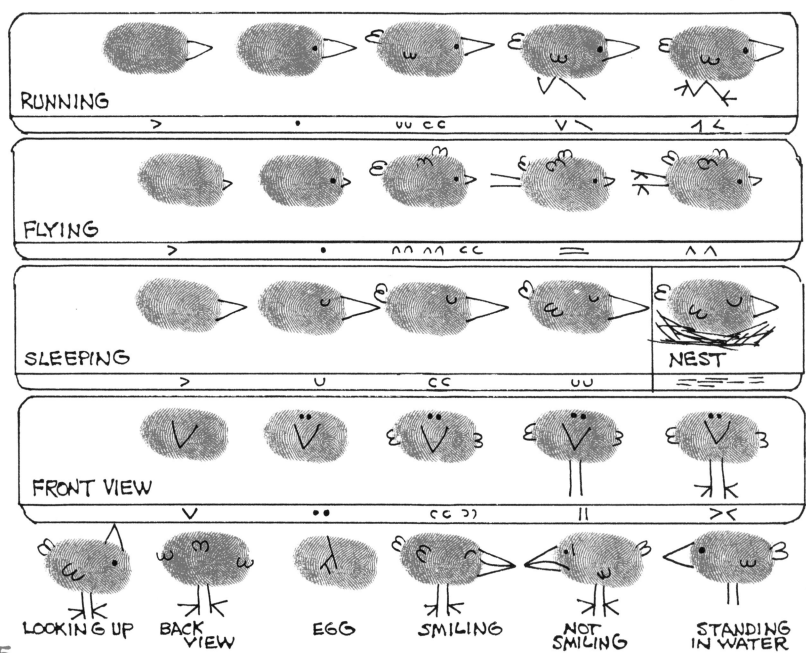

RUNNING

>   •   ʊʊ ᴄᴄ   ∨\   ↑↙

FLYING

>   •   ∩∩ ∩∩ ᴄᴄ   ═   ∧∧

SLEEPING

>   ∪   ᴄᴄ   ʊʊ

NEST

FRONT VIEW

∨   ••   (ᴄ))   ‖   ><

LOOKING UP   BACK VIEW   EGG   SMILING   NOT SMILING   STANDING IN WATER

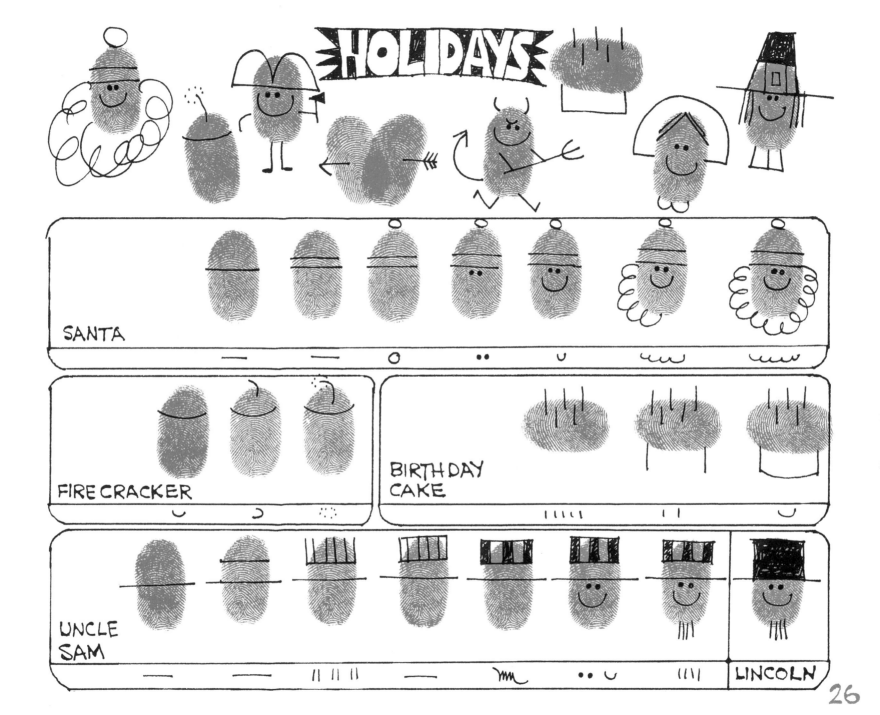

HOLIDAYS

SANTA

FIRE CRACKER

BIRTHDAY CAKE

UNCLE SAM

LINCOLN

26

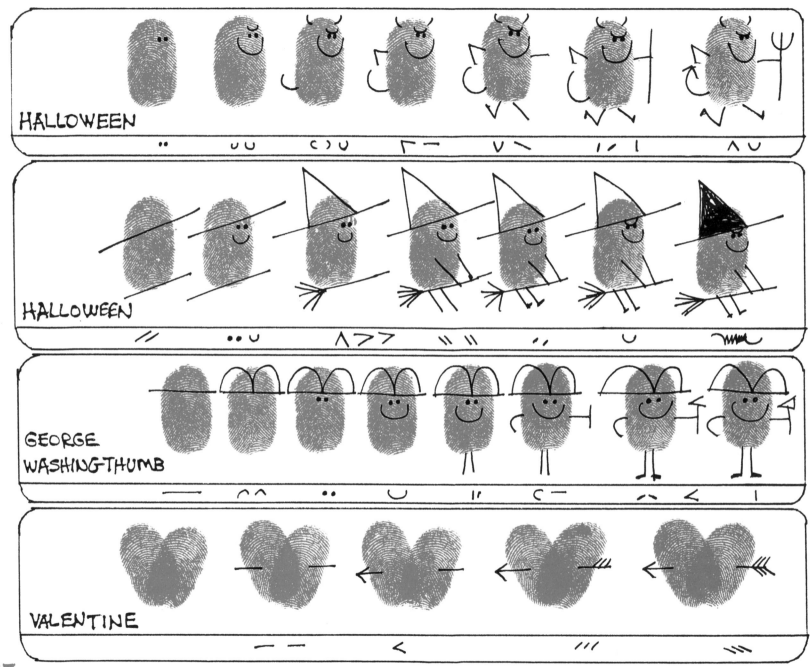

HALLOWEEN

HALLOWEEN

GEORGE
WASHING-THUMB

VALENTINE

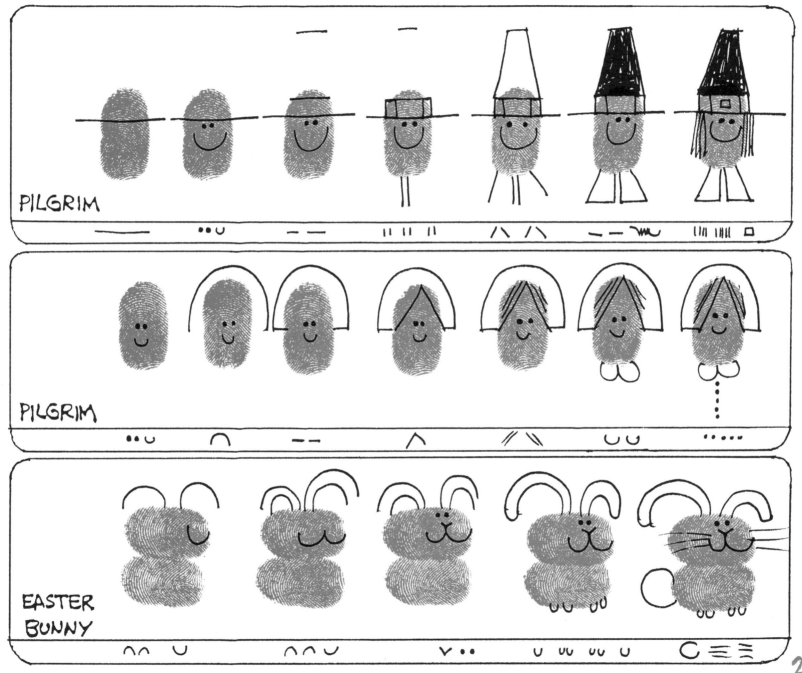

PILGRIM

PILGRIM

EASTER
BUNNY

28

FLOWERS

29

MORE THUMBS

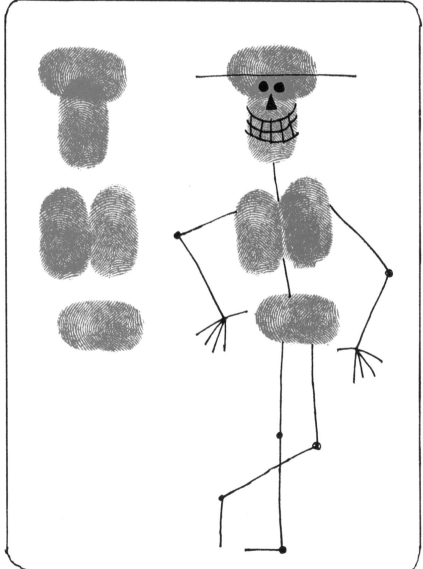

31

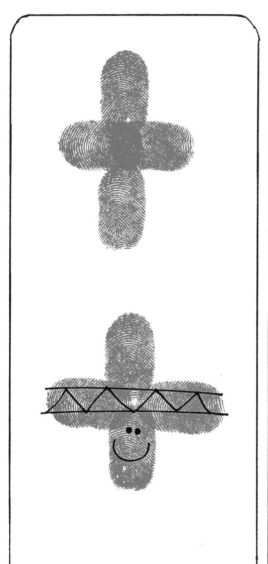

THIS AND THAT

33

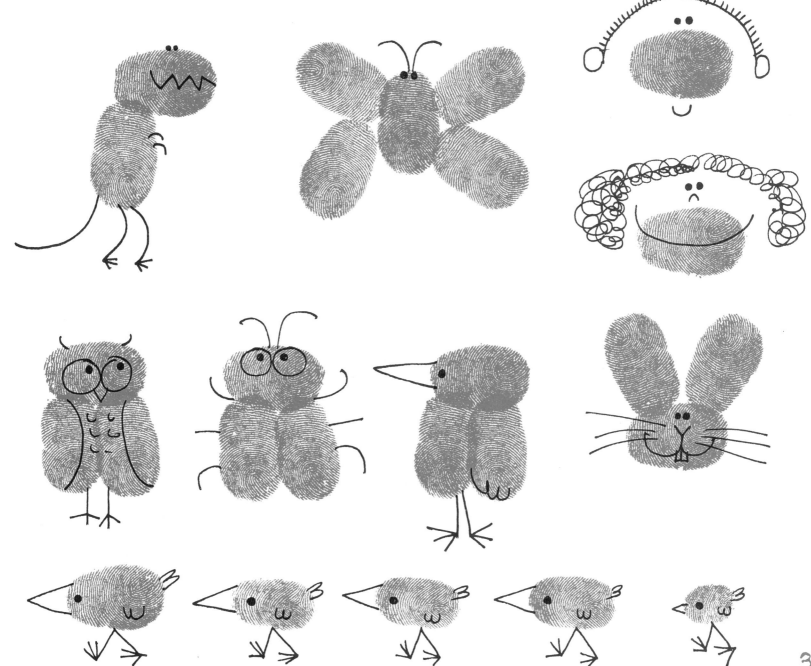

WAYS TO MAKE PRINTS

FOR THIS BOOK I USED A STAMP PAD I BOUGHT IN THE 5 AND 10.

A METAL
BOX.

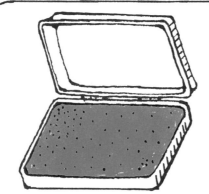

A DAMP,
INKY SPONGE
INSIDE.

I PRESSED
MY THUMB ON
THE PAD.

THEN I PRESSED
MY THUMB ON
THE PAPER —

I LET THE
PRINT DRY—

THEN I
DREW ON IT.

YOU CAN PAINT YOUR THUMB WITH WATER COLOR OR POSTER PAINT AND STAMP IT.

YOU CAN MAKE YOUR OWN PAD FROM A SPONGE OR A FOLDED CLOTH SOAKED WITH FROSTING COLOR.

YOU CAN USE A CUT CARROT OR POTATO.

CUT   PAINT   STAMP   DRY   DRAW

YOU CAN DRAW A ROUND SHAPE OR MAKE A BLOB.

BLOB   ROUND SHAPE   PAINTED THUMB   STAMP PAD   CARROT   POTATO

- THERE ARE MORE THAN 4 BILLION THUMBS IN THIS WORLD.
- NO TWO THUMBPRINTS HAVE <u>EVER</u> BEEN FOUND THAT ARE JUST ALIKE.
- THAT MEANS THAT THERE IS NO OTHER THUMBPRINT IN THIS WORLD EXACTLY LIKE YOURS.
- I THINK THAT MAKES YOUR THUMBPRINT SOMETHING SPECIAL!

Ed Emberley